Education on the Internet
A Student's Guide
• • • • • • •

By Andrew T. Stull

Adapted for Merrill Education by
Randall J. Ryder

Merrill,
an imprint of Prentice Hall
Upper Saddle River, New Jersey   *Columbus, Ohio*

Editor: Debra A. Stollenwerk
Developmental Editor: Carol S. Sykes
Production Editor: Mary Harlan
Marketing Coordinator Julie M. Shough
Design Coordinator: Julia Zonneveld Van Hook
Production Manager: Patricia A. Tonneman
Electronic Text Management: Marilyn Wilson Phelps, Matthew Williams, Tracey Ward

© 1997 by Prentice-Hall, Inc.
Simon & Schuster/A Viacom Company
Upper Saddle River, New Jersey 07458

This publication was adapted by Randall J. Ryder for Merrill Education from *Life on the Internet: Biology, A Student's Guide*, written by Andrew T. Stull to accompany *Biology: Life on Earth*, by Audesirk & Audesirk, © 1996 by Prentice Hall, Inc.

Printed in the United States of America
ISBN: 0-13-576208-1

TRADEMARK INFORMATION:
America Online is a registered trademark of Quantum Computer Services Incorporated. *CompuServe* is a trademark of CompuServe, Incorporated. *Delphi* is a trademark of Delphi Internet Services Corporation. *eWorld* is a trademark of Apple Computer Incorporated. *NCSA Mosaic* is a trademark of the National Center for Supercomputing Applications. *Netscape Navigator* is a registered trademark of Netscape Communications Corporation. *Prodigy* is a registered trademark of Prodigy Systems Incorporated. *Astound* is a registered trademark of Gold Disk. *Eudora* is a registered trademark of QUALCOMM Enterprise Software Technologies (QUEST). *Internet Explorer* is a registered trademark of Microsoft Corporation. *PowerPoint* is a registered trademark of Microsoft Corporation.

The author and publisher of this manual have used their best efforts in preparing this book. The author and publisher make no warranty of any kind, expressed or implied, with regard to these programs or the documentation contained in this book. The author and publisher shall not be liable in any event for incidental or consequential damages in connection with, or arising out of, the furnishing, performance, or use of the programs described in this book.

Contents

• • • • • • •

Introduction
O Brave New World
●●●●●●●
Brief Internet History

There are important things that history can teach you. If you don't learn them then you may find yourself walking into problems or even trouble that otherwise could have been avoided. Don't get me wrong, there is a lot of junk out there that is called history, but take a look at it first before you decide you don't really need it.

This thing that we now call the Internet has been around for just over twenty-five years and has been growing and changing ever since it first started. Its age is irrelevant for our discussion here, but the reasons for its creation and growth are quite interesting and helpful in understanding its nature, its terminology, and the culture of the people that have adopted it as home.

The Internet has been likened to something alive because of the way it grows and changes. The best description of the Internet is that it is not a network but a network of networks. In the late 50's and early 60's, scientists and engineers realized the importance of sharing and communicating through their computers. As things go, many different groups attempted to develop a network language and most were successful. The ironic thing was that now there were many different computer networks that still couldn't speak the same language. It was the Tower of Babel situation all over again.

The Internet was born as the solution to this problem. The US government paid for the development of a common network language (called a protocol) which was eventually shared freely. With time, the many isolated networks from all over the world adopted this language (called TCP/IP). There is no central Internet agency and therefore the Internet is independent of governments and regulation. It grows and changes from the common need and commitment of the people that use it.

Admittedly this type of network system isn't the most graceful—but it works. If you saw a diagram of this great big computer network you might easily recognize it as a spider's web. On this web, information can easily travel between any two points along many different paths. This web is called the "Internet" and it was born in 1969. Although the Internet is used very extensively for scientific purposes, as you can tell by the recent explosion of movies and commercials, it is growing for many other reasons!

The Internet is going through many changes in the way information is provided. Although its initial purpose was to allow a distributed system for scientific exchange and research, it gradually took on the role of digital post office (electronic mail and file transfer). As technology changed, the transfer speed and the way we viewed the information changed. Earlier work on the Internet relied on a "command-line interface," where a user simply typed commands from a keyboard and waited for the response. DOS controlled computers are an example of this. Recent advancements have brought us the graphical user interface (GUI). Macintosh and Microsoft Windows are classic examples of systems that use a GUI. These GUIs rely on icons and images to symbolize activities and commands. Actions are initiated with a mouse click instead of a typed command. One of the first commonly used GUIs for the Internet was *Gopher*, developed at the University of Minnesota in 1991. The title *Gopher* comes from the fact that UM's mascot is the *Gopher*. If you spend any time around computers, you might realize that computer hacks have a fondness for rodents. Actually, they have a fondness for cartoons and old movies too. When you get a chance, see if you can find the services *Archie, Veronica,* and *Jughead*.

Gopher is a visual tool for the Internet, where information is presented as a hierarchical listing of directories and files. The users jump from general directories at higher levels to more specific directories at lower levels until they find what they want. Beyond searching for information on a single computer, *Gopher* allows the users to quickly and transparently jump from one computer to another. This method of interaction no longer requires the users to log-on to each computer independently but rather allows them to wander or *browse* (the *Gopher* people call this process "burrowing") at will among the vast stores of information on the world's computers. Once the information is found, it can easily be downloaded to the user's computer. By simplifying the access and use of the Internet, the number of users and businesses has increased at astronomical rates. Amazing if you think about it! You could be on your computer in Toledo, Ohio, jumping from one screen to another and without realizing it you might find yourself in Hamburg, Germany, Mexico City, or Tokyo, Japan. Wham! And no airline tickets!

The next major tool for the Internet followed in 1992 with the creation of the *World Wide Web* information format, conceived and initiated at CERN, in Switzerland. Although *Gopher*, as an initial attempt at navigating the Internet, was a good GUI, it lacked visual appeal. Okay, *Gopher* was boring and mundane as a method of organizing information when compared to the Web.

Information on the Web is posted as a "page" and it may contain text, images, sounds, and movies. The organization of a page is much like any printed page in a book. There are the visual improvements but the major innovation is the use of *hypertext*. Hypertext, more specifically hypermedia, is the use of words *and* images as links or connecting points to different text, images, sounds, or movies on other computers throughout the world.

After the introduction of the Web, there was a dilemma: a great place to go but no easy way to get there. Kind of like the moon in the 60's. The one thing still lacking was a convenient program which would allow users to access the Web easily. This program, *Mosaic*, appeared in 1993 from the National Center for Supercomputing Applications (NCSA). Not only did it allow for the browsing of Web pages, but it added the ability to use other Internet resources such as E-mail, *Gopher*, and FTP. With the release of this browser, the Web has been growing faster than the speed of light. In 1991, Internet users were around 700,000. After *Mosaic* in 1993, the number increased to around 1.7 million. In early 1996 the estimate was more than 30 million. This phenomenal growth is attributed to the release of *Mosaic* and sister browsers like *Netscape*. Today the Internet is changing at staggering rates and becoming more readily available to the average person. Just listen to the computer jargon from the magazines, radio, television, or movies.

Chapter 1
The Mechanics

• • • • • • •

Navigation Strategies

READY. SET. GO! Do you remember hearing those words when you were a kid? I used to run foot races with my friends when I was young. The kid that yelled for the start would always jump the line before he called GO. I'd be slow off of the line in some races, fast in others, and occasionally I'd even win. But at the end of the race, it didn't matter because we'd all be happy and we'd do it again—possibly to a different finish.

In the real world, not everyone starts at the same time but that does NOT determine the finish. In a similar way, many of you are reading this manual having a lot of experience with computers, while others have none at all. To begin this chapter you should have your computer set up and operational, including the necessary software and an Internet connection. For those of you who are new to this race, fear not. I have included several resources in the Appendixes to help you get started. These resources include a description of the necessary equipment (Appendix I), a list of the leading software (Appendix II), and a list of companies that would be glad to help you connect to the Internet for a small fee (Appendix III). After you read them, you'll have an equal chance at the starting line.

There are a staggering number of computers, software, and connections that you can use to get onto the Internet. I have written this manual to include the general features common to some of the different computers and software packages that you may be using. In certain situations, I made a personal choice so that this manual didn't become too generic or void of personality. Most notably, I have illustrated this manual using examples from the *Netscape* 2.1 software. It is a very good browser and *free* to students, educators, and schools.

1.1 What Your Mechanic Never Told You

The software that you'll use to access the Net is commonly called a *client* or a *Web browser*. It functions on an information exchange model called a *Client-Server model* (Figure 1). In this way, a client (your Web browser software) will communicate with a *server* (other Web server software) on the Internet to exchange information. When referring to the Web, the information that your browser receives from the server is called a *page*.

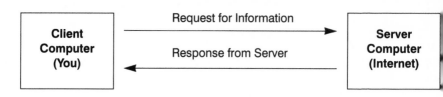

Figure 1
The client requests information from the server. The requested information is displayed on the client computer.

So, what really appears on these Web pages? The best way is to see for yourself. If you can, sit down in front of a computer, start your browser software, and connect to the Internet. Your browser is probably already set to start at a specific page. This start page is often referred to as a *homepage*. Web pages usually include both text and images. Some will also use sounds and videos. The use of different information types is called multi-media. When you choose a page it will be sent to your computer. After the requested information has been sent by the server, your computer will display it for you. As a basic rule, anything that can be saved or recorded onto a computer can be provided and distributed on the Internet through a Web page.

GoTo

Because sometimes it is better to begin by running before you know how to walk, I've put this section first. While the Internet may appear at first glance to be disorganized, finding your way around can be simplified by learning a few powerful tools. Once you become familiar with these tools finding your way through the Internet is really no harder than finding your way to a friend's house. Suppose that your friends are having a party at their new house and supplying all the entertainment and food. You're familiar with their town so you only need their address to get to the party. Navigating the Internet with a Web browser is even easier. If ou want to go someplace on the Web, all you do is type the address into he browser and connect to the desired page. No map required.

Information on the Internet has an address just as your friends do. Most browsers allow you the option of typing in an address and going directly to that document. With *Netscape,* there are two easy ways to do his. The easiest way is to use the *Open* toolbar button. A small window vill appear and offer you the opportunity to type in the address of the lesired document. A second method, and also one employed by other prowsers, is to modify the browser so that Internet addresses are view- ible.

With *Netscape,* you can open this window by selecting *Show Location* from the *Options* menu (Figure 2). The address window (see Figure 3) will appear immediately below the toolbar buttons. Just type in the requested addresses and press the return button on your keyboard.

Figure 2

Within *Netscape,* the selections under the *Option* menu act as tog- gle buttons. They can be alter- nately turned on (with a check mark) or off (without a check mark) by selecting them.

Figure 3

With the *Show Location* option selected in the *Option* menu the *Location* window will appear on your browser just below the toolbar.

Now that you know how to do it, here is an important address to get you started. This is the home page for the Prentice Hall text *Internet for Educators* (1997), which contains a multitude of links to Education resources on the Web.

http://execpc.com/~hughes

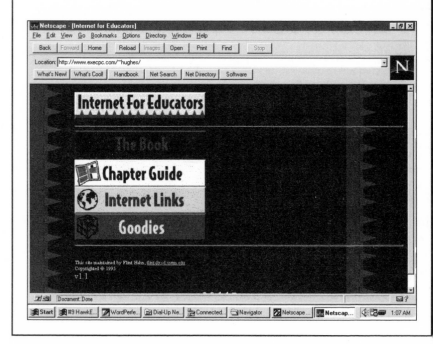

Navigation

You don't always have to know the address of a page to view it. The wonderful thing about the Web is that you can access (navigate) pages through the use of *hyperlinks*. Hyperlinks are a functional part of moving around the Web. You will notice these hyperlinks as colored words on the page. Images may also be hyperlinks. Your mouse is used to select or click on the desired hyperlink. Some Web authors write their pages so that their hyperlinks are hidden from you. If you are new, just click on everything. You can't break it.

With recent innovations in writing Web pages, other interactions are possible. Clickable images or maps are becoming a prominent way of interacting with Web pages. With a clickable image, you have the option to select/click a section on the image which functions as a hyperlink. This is different from the normal image link because the author of a Web page can connect one image to many different places. An example might be an image of an animal cell. The creator of such a document might place a hyperlink under each picture of the different cellular components so that your selection of different cellular components would take you to different pictures and information.

Here are two addresses that use a clickable map. The first is Virtual Tourist of Central America, and the second is the Exploratorium, an interactive museum.

http://www.vtourist.com/webmap/cam.htm
http://www.exploratorium.edu/

Not all browsers support clickable maps but most good *Web* authors will still provide the same choices using conventional hyperlinks.

Hyperlinks are great for navigating the Internet. However, there are many documents that don't incorporate hyperlinks. If you end up on one of these pages, you'll need another method of navigation or you'll be in trouble. This is very similar to driving though a neighborhood, turning the corner onto a dead end and realizing you don't have a reverse gear. The solution, of course, is to *have* a reverse gear. All good browsers incorporate basic features, such as *Back* and *Forward*, to allow the user to hop between recently viewed pages.

Although I'm using illustrations of the *Netscape* browser to illustrate points for the manual, you'll find that most browsers differ in the appearance only to the degree that their toolbar buttons for basic navigation are in different order (something you can handle). Figure 4 illustrates the basic orientation of the navigation buttons for *Netscape* 2.01.

Figure 4
The *Netscape* Navigator 2.01 Web browser offers a wide selection of basic navigation and control buttons at the toolbar. Although this is a representation of the control strip from the Windows version, the Macintosh version is identical in function and similar in appearance. The toolbars from other browsers offer similar functions.

One of the most useful features that you'll use is the *Home* button. This feature allows you to jump, just like Dorothy with her ruby slippers, back to your homepage. We'll discuss later in the manual how to choose and set your homepage. Two additional buttons that are common on most browsers are the *Reload* and *Stop* buttons. *Netscape* also includes many other features within its toolbar to give you flexibility in navigating the Internet, but they are self-explanatory and may differ from some of the options provided by other browser programs.

Don't wait until the last minute. Use one of the addresses I gave you and experiment with the buttons on your browsers. If you want something different, then give the following address a try.

http://www.yahoo.com/index.html

Yahoo! is a directory of information that was originated at Stanford University. Remember you won't break anything and if you get lost, you can always shut down the program, have lunch, and try again later!

Up to now, everything on a Web page has been described as a point, click, and jump. A new feature called *Forms* has added an entirely new dimension to both the user and the creator of Web pages. On some Web pages, you will find a section where you may be asked to give information by typing from the keyboard. This information might be in the form of a user survey, an answer to a question, or a request by you to a Web server. An example of the use of forms is the *BrainTainment Center* home page that contains a number of intelligence tests that you can complete on-line, then have your results displayed within a matter of seconds.

Experiment with some of the various assessment devices on the *BrainTainment Center* and amaze your friends and colleagues with your intellect! Remember not to take the results too seriously. After all, it is just an on-line test that purports to predict a narrow aspect of intelligence.

http://world.brain.com/

1.2   Return to Sender—Address Unknown

The addresses that you've been using on the Web are called Uniform Resource Locators or URLs for short. Each URL has a couple of basic parts just like a residential address. Look at some of the URLs (now you know what they are called) that you've used already. Do you notice any common features or similarities between them?

Here is yet another example of a typical URL and a pretty cool site in itself. There are three basic components to a URL. Compare this with the others I've given to you.

http://sln.fi.edu/tfi/hotlists/hotlists.html

Here are the three components:

protocol	http://
server	sln.fi.edu
path	tfi/hotlists/hotlists.html

It may seem confusing at first, but think of it as nothing more than a postal address squished together without any spaces. The protocol of the URL denotes how the information is stored. In the exercise above, "HTTP" refers to the protocol or language form which all Web servers speak. The colon and slashes are used to separate it from the name of the server. They are not always present with every type of URL. The path describes the location of the Web page on the server.

The last part of the server name defines the domain to which the server belongs. A domain is just a fancy name for a functional network group. The most common domain that you'll see is the .edu domain that encompasses educational institutions.

Some of the other domains you are likely to encounter are *com, gov, mil, net,* and *org.* Here are a couple of examples that you might be interested in. Can you determine what their domain represents?

http://aol.com
http://www.nps.gov/
http://navysgml.dt.navy.mil/patteam/wwwintro.html
http://envirolink.org/

One more thing, just so you can't say that I didn't tell you. In your travels, you will eventually jump to a server that is outside your country. Much, but not all, of the information on these servers is in English (so unless you are paying attention you might never know your foreign whereabouts). URLs of foreign servers have an additional section at the end of the servers name. It is a two letter code that denotes the country. Here are just a few examples but I trust that you can find more.

.au	Australia
.ca	Canada
.ch	Switzerland
.nl	Netherlands
.pe	Peru
.uk	United Kingdom

Up until this point, we have only been discussing browsers as an interpreter for documents that use hyperlinks. However, browsers also have the power to link to other, much older, formats of information that is available on the Internet. Let's look at two different URLs. The first is an FTP site, or a location where you will find a directory of files you can download to your computer. The second type of URL is a Gopher site which is limited to text displayed in black and white. Links to multiple FTP and Gopher sites can be found at the following location.

http://execpc.com/~hughes/links.html

I'm sure that most of you have done this but just to catch the loose ends I'd like the rest of you to visit the following site. This Web page of *Yahoo* contains a hyperlinked random generator designed to randomly drop you on a URL somewhere in the world. Simply click your mouse on the 'random' icon at the top of the page and you will be connected to a site.

http://www.yahoo.com

While you are out in the world, see if you can find URLs from other countries. Remember that you can always use your Back or Home button to return to the safety of home.

Bookmarks

Now that you've found so many *really* interesting pages, how do you find them again a day or a week from now? This is where bookmarks come in. You place a bookmark on the page to which you wish to return. Just to get your collection started, try this address: **http://www.hotwired.com**. It's the on-line version of Wired Magazine and a pretty interesting place. If you like their page, you can save a bookmark by selecting *Add Bookmark* from the *Bookmarks* menu on your browser (Figure 5). Some browsers may be different. *Mosaic* uses the term *Hotlist* instead of *Bookmark*, but the same general idea applies. Now, if you use your mouse to go back to the *Bookmarks* menu, you'll see that *Hotwired* is just a jump away. You don't have to memorize the URL and you don't have to haphazardly jump around until you find it again.

Figure 5
After you've added book-marks to your browser they will appear in a list under the *Bookmarks* menu on the menubar. Once you've selected a list of bookmarks you may use the *View Book-marks . . .* to arrange and organize them into categories.

Depending on the vintage of your browser, you may have the option of organizing your bookmarks in categories. Additionally, it is possible to export your bookmarks as a group so that you can give them to others. It's similar to trading baseball cards. I won't go into the procedures here, but as with life, it's yours, use it wisely, learn, and have fun.

Travel History

If you've been working along with your manual and your browser at the same time, you've probably been to many places on the Web. Obviously, if you want to move back and forth between your selections you are probably using the Forward and Back buttons on the browser's toolbar. But what do you do if you want to go back to someplace you've visited fifteen jumps ago? Do you press the Back button fifteen times? Well, if you choose to do it that way, *fine*, but it is a little slow. Computer hacks are lazy sometimes and using the back button fifteen times would drive them crazy (excuse me, that's crazier); so there's a great feature that allows you to jump rapidly to any of the places you've visited along your path of travel. If you are using the Netscape browser then click on the *GO* menu option and you'll see a list of all of the places you've visited on your journey. Other browsers have similar features. The simple point is that if you don't want to use the Back button fifteen times, you can select from a list of recently viewed pages.

Now that you've got the hang of it, give the following URLs a try. I picked some that I thought were interesting but you'll find many more. Have fun.

http://espnet.sportszone.com/
ESPN Sports
http://www.foxnetwork.com/home.html
FOX Broadcasting Company
http://www.iuma.com/iuma/indes_graphic.html
Independent Underground Music Archive
http://www.mtv.com/index.html
MTV (Music Television)
http://www.nbc.com/index.html
NBC (National Broadcasting Company)
http://www.nflhome.com/index.html
NFL (National Football League)
http://www.pathfinder.com/
Time Warner Communications (*Life, People, Sports Illustrated* and more)

When you find something that you think is fun and interesting, save it or give it to a friend.

●●●●●●●●
Activity

365 Adventures Without Ever Leaving Home

I hope that you haven't waited until this point to travel the Web but if you have, this exercise will get you up to speed. You'll have plenty of opportunity to experience some of the great places that are at your disposal on the Internet. The only thing that you'll need is the knowledge of reading URLs and saving bookmarks.

What you'll be doing is touring various worldwide news sources on the Internet. Rather than the URLs for each of these sites, you will find a comprehensive set of links listed on Trib.Com News. With each *news source* you connect to, check the URL.

http://www.trib.com/news/
Trib.Com News

This exercise is really a free ride. I hope that you'll experience many different places and discover some that have value to you. If you find something that you like, set a bookmark or record the URL so that you can return.

1. Compile a list of the different countries you visit. I've given you a basic set of country domain codes. How many more can you find?
2. How many foreign languages can you find? English is probably the most common but definitely not the only one you'll encounter.

Netscape and many other browsers allow you to organize bookmarks into categories. I haven't described how to do this but you can find the information in on-line user manuals. It's not hard. I use categories like: *Fun and Games, Magazines, News and Weather, Outdoors,* and *Science.* Under each of these major categories I have sub-categories. Using Science as an example, I have sub-categories like: *Botany, Marine Biology, Museums, Newsgroups, Zoology,* etc . . . And if you want a bookmark system that has categories and links already established, check out *SmartMarks,* a program you can download from Netscape Corporation (http://www.netscape.com).

3. Organize your bookmarks into categories so that they are easy to use. Use the categories that I've described above or you can make your own.

Chapter 2
Caught in the Net

• • • • • • •

Education Resources

In Chapter 1 you learned what the Internet is, how to use a browser, and what resources are available to you through the Web. If you've done your homework, you'll also realize that you have no chance of ever memorizing the content or location of everything at your disposal. This leads us into our next major point. Since you have no hope of ever memorizing all of that information, then your best bet is to learn how to *find* information when you need it. This chapter also presents you with Web resources that can be used in an educational setting. Furthermore, within the chapter, I will show you a few tricks to allow you to search the Web for just about any information you may wish to obtain. If you remember, the first chapter really covered the technique of browsing, which is just the haphazard wandering from one place to another. Here, you will learn to search actively for specific information.

2.1   Second Floor! Washers. Dryers. Kitchen Sinks.

If you really think about it, you'll realize that change is a central theme of Education. Recognizing that it's important to try to provide the most current and accurate information in a changing world, we will examine a variety of hypertext resources on the Web. These resources will provide you information in the form of graphics, text, audio, video, and downloadable software.

- **Graphics**
  The Web contains graphic information in a variety of forms including photographs, drawings, computer generated art, and live images that are captured with digital photography and presented in the form of a motionless image. Here is an annotated list of just a few sites containing a variety of graphic images:

Weathernet

http://cirrus.sprl.umich.edu/wxnet/

A rather amazing site! Here you will find color and black and white photos and satellite imagery of weather formations throughout the world. The site also displays recent radar images of any location in the United States.

World Museums

http://www.cgrg.ohio-state.edu/newark/museums.html

This site provides links to hundreds of museums around the world. Many of the museums provide for visual tours of the museum in the form of colorful graphic images.

Virtual Hospital

http://indy.radiology.uiowa.edu/virtualhospital.html

Not for the faint hearted. This site presents graphic images of various parts of the body and the effect of various diseases on body organs and tissues.

Images on the Web can be saved and reproduced in various forms. The most simple procedure to save an image is to print it as it is being displayed on your monitor. This process will vary according to the type of operating system your computer uses so check your operating system user manual for specific directions on printing from your screen. A second form for saving images is to save them on your hard drive or a fixed disk. Again, the process for saving screens (also called screen dumps) varies with operating systems, so again check your user manual. Once saved on a file, however, these images can be inserted into word processing documents, presentation software such as Microsoft's *PowerPoint* or Gold Disk's *Astound,* or they can be printed on your color or gray scale printer.

- **Text**

  Clearly there is a considerable source of information on the Web available in text format. In fact, some sites actually allow you to download sizeable files. There are a variety of sites that are rich resources to locate text on various topics. Among these sites are libraries, sites that contain on-line periodicals and journals, and entire books. Again, here are a number of sites offering a variety of information in the form of text.

  Library of Congress-Internet Resource Page

  http://lcweb.loc.gov/global/gov.html

Hundreds of text documents from the legislative, judicial, and executive branch of government as well as documents from foreign governments, states, and the military.

Project Gutenberg

http://www.nlc-bnc.ca/ifla/services/gutenberg/ gutnberg.htm

Complete version of hundreds of books. Here you can download *The Red Badge of Courage, Peter Pan, The Scarlet Letter, A Tale of Two Cities* and other great classics.

Text can be saved or edited in a variety of ways. The most direct process is to save the text using the save command from your browser. If you use *Netscape,* simply go to the top of the screen, click on FILE and then select "save as". The program will then ask you for a name to assign to the file and where you would like to view the file. Once saved, you can examine the file by clicking on the name of the file in the directory where it has been placed. Once you have selected this file, *Netscape* is activated (even though you may not be on-line) and the file can then be viewed just as though you were connected to the Web although everything you view on your screen is actually information saved on your computer. Another procedure to save text is to use your mouse to click, then highlight the text displayed on your screen. Next, go to the top of the screen, click on EDIT and COPY the file. It has now been saved on your clipboard and can be pasted into your word processing program. Finally, text can also be obtained on the Web by downloading text files from FTP sites. One of these sites, Project Gutenberg, for example, allows you to download hundreds of complete books.

- **Audio**
  The Web can act as a radio station, a telephone, and as a cassette player. If you have a sound card installed in your computer you can "listen" to live broadcasts, talk with people around the world (at no cost), and download sound files that can later be played. Using these tools requires special software that can be downloaded at no cost. For more information on the use of this software and its capabilities, connect to the following Web sites.

  RealAudio

  http://www.realaudio.com
  This site will explain the uses of the RealAudio player and direct you to sites where you can listen to on-line audio broadcasts. The software allowing you to play audio on the Net cab also be obtained at this site.

Stoutman's Wave Sounds

http://www.stoutman.qbd.com/

This site contains numerous sound files that you can download, then play on *Netscape* and other browser programs.

Internet Phone **by VocalTec**

http://www.vocaltec.com

Yes, you can reduce long distance charges if you and the party you wish to speak to have a copy of *Internet Phone* and a sound card. This site explains the use of *Internet Phone* and allows you to download the free software version.

- **Video**

  Yes, the Web allows you to receive video in black and white as well as color. You can also broadcast video on the Web in black and white with the use of a very small camera that can be purchased for less than $100. While the quality of the video is not as good as your television, this is a rapidly developing aspect of the Web. Undoubtedly, advances in the use of video on the Web will improve rather quickly. Information on using video can be obtained from the following sites.

  CU-SeeMe

  http://magneto.csc.ncsu.edu/multimedia/classes/ spring94/projects/proj6/

  Here you will find detailed descriptions of the use of the *CU-SeeMe* software and links to download the software. By attaching an inexpensive camera and activating this software, you will have the capability of broadcasting almost real time video around the world.

- **Software**

  Wow! There is a tremendous amount of software available on the Web. Quite literally you have access to hundreds of thousands of software programs that can be downloaded to your computer's hard drive or fixed disk. Many are educational software designed for classroom instruction. This software is available for numerous operating systems such as Windows, Macintosh, OS-2, and DOS. The most efficient means of locating and downloading software is connecting to the site Shareware.com which will direct you to over 170,000 software programs. Connect to this site and select the browse command to see the most popular programs, or use the search command to locate software that would be useful in your classroom.

http://www.shareware.com

2.2   Let Your Fingers Do the Walking

While the Web is an information jungle, locating that information can be a challenge. The locational tools that I'll describe here are free and easy to use, but you should remember that searching for information on the Internet or elsewhere is a skill that needs to be practiced.

There are two types of tools that you'll use most often to search for information. These are directories and search engines.

Directories

Directories are sites on the Web that have indexed information similar to the table of contents of a book. *Yahoo!* (http://www.yahoo.com) is only one of many directories that are available in the Internet but it is the best for general topics. As you become more experienced and traveled in the Web you will discover more. I didn't name it and I don't know why it's called that but it is easy to remember. As I describe this tool, I'd like you to follow along and experiment with it.

Yahoo! is a listing of information by category—kind of like a card catalog. At the top of the listing, there are several very general categories, but as you move deeper into the directory you'll notice that the categories become more specific. To find information, you simply choose the most appropriate category at the top level and continue through each successive level until you find what you're looking for or until you realize you're in the wrong place. Don't worry, I get lost most of the time.

As an example, suppose you were attempting to learn more about the use and impact of technology in Education. Within *Yahoo!*, notice that one of the top level categories is Education. After accessing the Education category, you'll notice that it gives a list of many different categories. So, what is your next choice? My choice is Instructional Technology and Training. Because *Yahoo!* cross references among the categories, you'll find that several related categories will lead you to your desired page.

Much of your success in finding information with this type of tool really centers around your preparation for the search. Often, it is possible to find information on a topic in a category that may at first seem unrelated to your topic of interest. Again, let's take the example of technology in Education. Although you may consider this to be a topic to be searched out from a category in Education, there are other avenues to consider. For example, the category of science will contain information of the development of technology from a scientific standpoint, and certainly the category of social science will contain information on the impact of technology on people and their cultures.

Prepare yourself for a search *before* you jump into one. In the long run it will save you both time and frustration. Don't be afraid to try some strange approaches in your search strategy. A good technique that I use occasionally is to pull out my thesaurus and look up other names for the word. It may be that you can find a more common form of the word. Think of all the associations that your query may have and give them each a try. You never know when it will turn up a gold mine.

Search Engines

Another more direct approach to finding information on the Web is to use what is called a Search Engine. Don't be confused by the term. It is nothing more than a program that runs a search for you while you're waiting for the results. There are many search engines on the Web. Recently, over a hundred types of search engines have been placed on one site allowing you to readily switch from one search engine to another. This site, called *All-In-One Search Page* (http:www.albany.net/all inone/all1www.html#www) is a useful source for conducting searches on topics, people, spelling, and even quotations. Some of the Web search engines are commercial and they may charge you a fee to run a search. Just as anything that proves itself to be in demand, the Web is turning commercial and you will notice many places will begin as a free service and eventually ask you to pay a fee. Don't worry, there are plenty of free search engines and many more popping up all the time.

A search engine that I use frequently is called *AltaVista* (http://altavista.digital.com). It's very simple to operate but as with any search tool, it takes practice and patience to master. Take a few moments and connect to *AltaVista* and we'll take it for a test run. When you first see the opening page, you'll notice that it is very simple. Fear not, behind this page is a very good resource. Reading the instructions on the page will tell you most everything you need to know. Enter a word into the white entry box and press the submit button; *AltaVista* will refer back to its database of information and return a page of hyperlinked resources containing the word you entered. When the query results come back to you, notice that they are hyperlinks to somewhere out on the Web.

Both as an example of how a search engine works and as a comparison with *Yahoo!*, use "technology" as topic for the search. Notice that you can set the number of responses that the engine will return to you. How do the search engine results compare with *Yahoo!*? Did you notice that some of your results didn't seem to apply to your topic? If you said yes, then you've noticed one of the downfalls of search engines. They are very fast and very dumb. They don't think (that is your job). A search using the term "technology" is just as likely to turn up a link to a rock band or the name of a commercial establishment as a link to the impact of technology on our society. To perform an effective search you will need to spend time *before* the search preparing a search strategy. When you perform a search using an automated tool like a search engine you can expect many links to be unrelated to your intended topic—but all-in-all they are very powerful tools that are constantly becoming more efficient.

With all of the experience that you've accumulated, why don't we put it to a test. I'll give you several words or phrases that are related to Education, and you try to find something related to them using *Yahoo!,* and *AltaVista.* Once you've exhausted these tools then try the URL that I've provided for you at the bottom of this box. Think of it as a game—like the fox and hounds. Do you have the skills to get the information before others in your class?

School Finance	Inclusion
Cooperative Learning	School Reform

http://www.infoseek.com/home

Activity

The Great Cyberspace Hunt

Here's what you've all been waiting for! I've been keeping my ear close to the ground listening for information on education in the popular press and media. The first list is a set of Education-related terms that have become popular. See what you can find on these topics. Try to find the information in the least number of jumps possible. How are each of these terms influencing the human condition?

Zone of Proximal Development	Cooperative Learning
Advance Organizers	Constructivism
Information Processing	Metacognition
Multiple Intelligences	Schema Theory
IDEA (Individuals with	Misconceptions
Disabilities Education Act)	Inclusion

In addition to the terms listed above, I've included a list of Education researchers and theorists from this century. Some of them may be easier to track down than others. It has been a very interesting experience for me just to find the right people to include. I hope you'll find both their research and their lives interesting.

Your assignment is to put together a brief history of each Education researcher or theorist and their important contributions to Education. If you'd really like a challenge, try to draw a thread of connection between each to the others, no matter how thin or obscure. (Hint: To help you understand the challenge task, you should search out the term *Concept Map*).

David Ausubel	Howard Gardner
Jerome S. Bruner	John Goodlad
John Dewey	John Nussbaum
Rosalind Driver	Jean Piaget
Elliott Eisner	Louise Rosenblatt
Robert Gagné	Lev Vygotsky

Remember to use all of the resources at your disposal. Begin with the *Yahoo!* Directory and *AltaVista* search engine; then move on to some of the others that are provided in the *All-In-One* search group. Check the obscure as well as the popular resources. Don't be afraid to read ahead to Chapter 3 and use e-mail and newsgroup resources. You never know.

Chapter 3
Doing Your Own Tune-up

• • • • • • •

Advanced Techniques

I'm sure that by now you understand the direction of this manual. In Chapter 1 you were introduced to the depth and breadth of the Web. Through several exercises I helped you to wander and drift with the hope that you'd understand the potential of the resource you have at your disposal. Some may say that this was like Moses in the desert but I hope that it was more like a kid in a candy store. In Chapter 2, I introduced you to the skills you'd need to walk your own path. Due to the disorganized nature of the Web, effective searching is vital if you wish to tame the Web for purposeful study. This last chapter will cover some of the advanced techniques to help you make your Web experience more enjoyable and profitable.

I've illustrated this manual with *Netscape Navigator* 2.01 because I feel that it is the best browser on the market independent of the fact that it is free to education. Even though I've chosen *Netscape,* I encourage you to make up your own mind. You may find that another is more appropriate for you. Whatever you choose, the following descriptions and tech-

So that you have something for comparison, here are the home-pages for the two most prominent Web browsers, *Netscape* and the Microsoft *Internet Explorer.* They are free if you are a student or work with a school. Within these pages you will also find the manuals for each program.

Netscape
http://home.netscape.com/
Microsoft *Internet Explorer*
http://www.microsoft.com

niques should still help. Remember, the Web adventure is not in *what* you use, but *how* you use it.

3.1   I Prefer It <u>My</u> Way!

Know your options and you'll save both time and money. On the Internet, and as a matter of fact, in life, "Time is money." According to Einstein, "Time is relative," so I guess you could also say—"Time is relative to the amount of money you have." I wonder if Einstein thought of this? No, I'm not rambling. Here is where I get to the point. If you are like me, you don't have much money and time is very relative if you have to use a modem and a service provider to surf. If you know what your browser can and cannot do, and if you configure the options for your browser so that it is most efficient for you, you will save oodles of time. With *Netscape*, under the *Options* menu (Figure 6) you are allowed several choices to customize the appearance and function of your browser. I'll say it again, don't wait for me. Try these techniques as you go along and jump around to the information that is important to you.

Figure 6

Many of the general options are listed in the *Options* menu on *Netscape,* but if you wish to do a more detailed configuration, you can find more options under the *Preferences . . .* submenu.

I described some of these options previously and you may have already experimented with the others but here is an explanation for the rest of you. Notice that there is a check mark by some of the options. Look at *Auto Load Images* as an example. When the check is present, images will be automatically loaded. If you select this option again, the check mark disappears and subsequently, pages will load the text without the time-consuming images. Give it a try. If you're trying to connect to the Internet through a modem, as I frequently do, you've probably noticed that some of those images, sounds, and videos take a long time to download to your computer. This, in itself, isn't a big deal until you consider that some pages are crammed with images and downloading them requires a lot of time. This really digs into your wallet if you pay an hourly connection rate to your service provider. What I do to save some money and frustration is to turn off the automatic image load on my

---

The following is the URL for the *Netscape* handbook. You should refer to it whenever my ramblings stop making sense to you. You will also find other resources that will help you so don't hesitate to give it a look.

http://home.netscape.com/assist/support/client

---

browser until I get to a place of interest. In a similar fashion, the other options from this pull-down menu work much the same.

If this isn't enough control for you, there are other changes you can make. Notice the *Preferences . . .* sub-menu under *Options* (Figure 7). When you select this, you will be presented with a dialog window, where you can make even more customizing options. If you don't like the way the font, color, or style of the text appears on your browser, you can change them within this dialog window. Browsers typically provide you with many features to allow you to change the visual appearance of the information on the viewed page.

After opening the *Preferences . . .* dialog window, you will notice a couple of words in a box near the top of the window just to the left of a black triangle. This is called a pull-down box. If you click on the box a list of options will appear for you to select from. Each of these options will take you to a different preference window. Figure 7 lists the categories you have to select from when customizing your browser. This dialog window usually opens to the category you were last modifying, so don't be disoriented when it looks different each time.

One of the first preferences that you might want to modify is the location of your homepage. A homepage is sort of like home plate in baseball. It is the place where you begin your trip around the bases. If you're working with a browser that hasn't been customized before, it probably has the homepage set to the company that made it. If you're working on one of your school's computers, then the homepage may already be set to the school's page. If neither is the case, then within the *Appearance* preference window (Figure 8) you have the option to desig-

Figure 7
There are many choices available to you from within the *Preferences* sub-menu.

nate a homepage. By now you've probably found something on the Web that you are willing to call home. Enter the URL as illustrated below and every time you start your browser or select Home from the toolbar you'll end up at this URL. Later in this chapter we'll discuss how you can make and display your own homepage. Stay tuned. Notice that you also have the option of modifying the appearance of your toolbar.

On the *Appearance* preference window you also have the option of customizing the appearance of your hyperlinks. Hopefully, you've noticed that hyperlinks are normally blue (this is if you or someone else hasn't changed the default color). Once you've accessed them, they change to purple. This follows the bread crumb principle. It lets you know that you've already been down that link and therefore you should select a different path. You can set the length of time for a hyperlink before it changes back to the default color. Although the default is usually 30 days (Figure 8), I have my link expiration set to one day. Notice that you can have the browser underline the hyperlinks or leave them plain.

If you select the *Fonts* preference window you will see a dialog window (Figure 9) that will allow you to modify the font style and size of the text as displayed by your browser. If you typically have a difficult time reading small text from a computer screen, then you may want to increase the size or style of the font.

Figure 8
Your browser is easily customized to display your toolbar and homepage preferences.

Figure 9
Selecting a font of appropriate style and size will help you prevent eye strain and muscle fatigue from leaning over your computer to read.

As with fonts, the default text, hyperlink, and background colors can be modified on your browser to meet your individual desires (Figure 10). My suggestion is for you to set the colors so that you maximize the contrast between the components. Of course, you may choose to color your text the same color as your hyperlinks just to cause you more chaos in navigating a page.

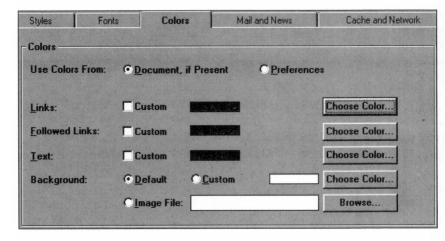

Figure 10
Customizing the colors of the components on your browser will help you quickly identify hyperlinks and navigational paths as you travel.

I have not covered all of the options available to you for customizing your browser. An extensive explanation is available to you through the *Netscape* homepage. If you are using another browser, you will find that they have similar options and on occasion some browsers may give you more power to control your browser's appearance. Again, it doesn't matter which browser *you* choose to use. All I have to say is, *To thine own self be true*. Okay, I want to say one more thing, *May the force be with you, young Skywalker*. I've always wanted to say that.

3.2   Do You Get the News Delivered?

Contrary to what you might be thinking, learning is a give-and-take activity. It is an interchange of ideas. Effective learning involves communication between all those involved—instructors and students. This means that students need to learn how to communicate among themselves. Within any learning environment, everyone brings a different and unique perspective. With the interchange of ideas, experiences, and understandings shared by each person, the whole community benefits. This brings me to my next point. *Netscape* and many other browsers have incorporated the ability to allow you to communicate through e-mail, newsgroups, and on-line interest groups.

E-mail

As we've discussed earlier, e-mail is the electronic exchange of mail among people. This exchange is from one person to another person. E-mail follows a similar Client-Server model as do Web browsers and Web servers. Your client software asks a server computer for new items of mail addressed to you. Your mail server is operated and maintained by the administrator of your campus or service provider. Where Web servers speak a computer protocol called HyperText Transport Protocol (HTTP), mail servers speak a computer protocol called Simple Mail Transport Protocol (SMTP). Another analogy for you: the server is like your mailbox. The mailbox is where mail addressed to you is stored until you pick it up. You use your mail client to get your mail from your mailbox.

E-mail links are built within many Web pages and allow you to send directed correspondence to other participants through the Internet. Although *Netscape* allows you to send e-mail to others, it doesn't allow you to receive e-mail. There are other pieces of software that allow you to receive e-mail. *Eudora* is one of these pieces of software; you may have heard of others. As with *Netscape*, *Eudora* has a free version and it is available for both Macintosh and Windows. Manuals that describe its use are common and easily available over the Internet. Some commercial browsers come with the ability to both send and receive e-mail but they may cost a little more money.

If you follow this URL you'll end up on the QualComm homepage where you can download either the free version of *Eudora* or get information on the more powerful commercial version. You can also download a copy of the basic user manual.

http://www.qualcomm.com/main/contacts.html

The following URLs are Web-based *Eudora* manuals. Remember to save a bookmark.

http://www.soc.staffs.ac.uk/eudora/contents.html

Access to an e-mail server is easily available. If you are at a campus that has provided you with Internet access, you should also have the ability to apply for an e-mail account through your campus computer administration. Again, if you haven't enrolled in an enlightened school, then you have the option of applying for an e-mail account through an independent service provider. In fact, if you've already gone through a service provider for access to the Internet, you probably already have e-mail capabilities. There are two things that you'll need to know to properly configure your browser for sending e-mail: (1) your e-mail address, (2) the name of your mail server. You can enter your e-mail information through the *Preferences . . .* sub-menu under *Options*. Once you open the Preferences dialog window, you should select *Mail and News* from the pulldown box. Figure 11 illustrates the appearance of the dialog window that will appear. Once you've entered the correct information and restarted the browser program, you should have the ability to send e-mail. Think about it! It means saving postage and long distance phone calls.

Styles	Fonts	Colors	**Mail and News**	Cache and Network

Mail

Mail (SMTP) Server:	your.mail.server
Your **N**ame:	Your Real Name
Your **E**mail:	Yourname@mail.server
Your **O**rganization:	Name of Your School
Signature File:	[ ] [Browse...]
Send and Post:	◉ Allow **8**-bit ○ Mime Compliant (**Q**uoted Printable)

Figure 11
The information about your particular mail server and e-mail address must be entered before you have the ability to send e-mail to others through *Netscape*.

E-mail addresses typically take a very distinctive format. Here is the format of a typical e-mail address: NAME@HOST.DOMAIN. It is not necessary to have a full name for the NAME part of the address, and in fact, some addresses use only numbers to represent an individual. The @ symbol always follows the individual's name and then the name of the mail server computer (HOST). The domain in the e-mail format, just like the domain of the URL format, is used to denote the affiliation of the user. Notice that there are no spaces anywhere in an e-mail address.

Here is an example of a typical e-mail address. There are three basic components to a typical e-mail address.

AStull@biology.fullerton.edu

Here are the three components:

individual	AStull
mail server	biology.fullerton
domain	edu

If you've read the title page to this manual, you'll realize that this is my e-mail address. I may regret it by putting it here but your comments and suggestions *are* important. Drop me a brief note if you have some suggestions for making this manual better. (E-mail addresses are not case sensitive. I use capitals so that addresses are easier to translate.)

Newsgroups

A second feature incorporated by many browsers is the ability to exchange ideas over something called Netnews or Newsgroups. A newsgroup is a group of people that connect to and participate in a specialized discussion. These groups are open forums and all are welcome to contribute in the interchange. Some are moderated by an individual or individuals that will post items for discussion and moderate the electronic brawls that ensue. Others are free-form and function much more like a street fight. The bottom line with all newsgroups is to have a central place where people can bring to the table new ideas and perspectives. No, not all newsgroups are places for disagreement. Many are very good, with courteous people and polite conversation.

Newsgroups are nearly the opposite of e-mail. Where e-mail is sent and posted for a single person to read, news postings are sent to a common place for all to read and comment. By now you've noticed that I like using analogies. Here is yet another analogy that will help you understand the nature of a newsgroup. If e-mail is like the postal service, newsgroups are like coffee houses on open microphone night.

Okay, so what is the purpose of the newsgroups if people just contribute ideas and comments to a mass discussion on a particular topic?

Newsgroups are a place where you can go and ask questions, get ideas, and generally learn about specifics. Select a group that has an interest common to yours or a topic where you are trying to learn something. You'll find that there are many newsgroups that focus on issues of Education (and everything else that a human mind could think of).

The names of newsgroups are usually descriptive of their discussion topic. There are several major newsgroup categories. The one you'll use most is the *K12* group. This group contains various Education discussions. An easy way to access Education newsgroups is to use the *Internet for Educators* Web page. Simply click on the newsgroups as shown below, and the newsgroup reader will be activated and display the contents of the newsgroup you have selected. It is that easy! You will also find a list of Education newsgroups in Appendix IV.

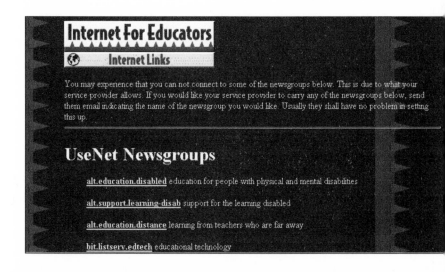

To configure your browser to connect to a newsgroup, you will need the name of the server computer that handles newsgroups. This may or may not be the same computer that handles your e-mail and Web services. News servers use yet another protocol beyond HTTP and SMTP. News servers use a protocol called NetNews Transfer Protocol or NNTP. To keep away feelings of being overwhelmed, on donut day, take a couple of the really sugary donuts down to your local hack and don't forget the coffee. There is nothing you can't get out of a hack with a little sugar and caffeine.

Once you have an e-mail address, the name of your mail server (SMTP server), and the name of your news server, you're set. If you are using *Netscape*, you can configure your browser by selecting *Preferences* from the *Option* menu. Within the Preferences window that appears, you must select *Mail and News* from the pull-down option box and then enter your information.

Here is an example of a typical newsgroup URL. Newsgroup names are divided into several descriptive words separated by a period and organized into a hierarchy. Notice that newsgroup URLs don't use the double slash (//).

news:k12.chat.teacher

Here are the three components:

protocol	news:
top category	k12
sub category	chat
sub category	teacher

The only way to really understand what newsgroups are like is to try them. Here are a couple of newsgroups that will get you started. Connect to one of interest and read some of the postings. You can find a larger list in Appendix IV. For your first time, you should just read the postings and follow some of the conversations. Connections or threads develop between postings as people add comments to earlier postings. As you become familiar with the topic of discussion you might post a comment yourself.

news:k12.chat.elementary
news:k12.chat.senior
news:k12.sys.projects

To get the real flavor of a newsgroup you need to spend more than just a couple of minutes viewing one. Choose a newsgroup of interest. Within that newsgroup select a topic that is being discussed and follow it for a week. As a discussion grows, you'll notice that many people will jump in to participate.

3.3 There's No Place Like Home

There *is* no place like home. You may or may not have found some place on the Web that you are willing to call home, but if you haven't found one, then hopefully you'll be able to use the following description to create one for yourself. It is not as simple as browsing the Web *but* it's not very hard either. If your campus has a Web server, then they may have a place for student homepages. Ask around to see if you are allowed to keep a homepage there. If you can't get access through your campus, you still have other options. Some of the pages that you view on your browser reside on a Web server, but you can also create a file on your home computer or even on a floppy disk that will act as a homepage for you. Admittedly, in order for your homepage to be on the Internet, you'd need access to a Web server; but it's not necessary for the basics that I'll describe here. Another option is to use a private service provider to gain access to the Internet. Some service providers rent space to keep homepages on their server. One of the latest things to be expanding is the idea of the Internet Coffee House. There are several that have just opened up. They'll serve up great coffee and provide you with access to the Web. Some have even gone as far as renting space for homepages. Search one out.

Homepages

Homepage this and homepage that. What good is a homepage? You will find other uses but here are a couple of reasons I keep a homepage. I use a homepage to organize my important and frequently accessed links and bookmarks to the Internet. Most importantly, these are links and bookmarks to Education resources all over the world. It's better than a library card. I also keep links to on-line magazines, the weather at my favorite camping spots, movie, music, and book reviews, the current news reports, my school's homepage, my friends' pages (only the cool ones), the manuals for my e-mail and Web clients, and my favorite search engines and directories. I've even seen students create hyperlink pages that they gave to their instructors as homework assignments. Imagine turning in an assignment where your instructor could use a Web browser to link to your references and resources on the Internet. I wanted to keep a picture of my mom on my homepage but she didn't like the fact that millions of people could see it. You better ask yours too. My homepage also has a little about me. I'd like to think that it reflects a personality that's not boring, dull, or generic (although some have said that that *is* my personality).

Now, where is yours? Actually, I've already made one for you. All you have to do is add the stuff about yourself and the links that you think are cool and interesting. Once you've done that, it's all downhill. If you look at Appendix V, you'll see that there is a lot of gibberish that may or may not look like computer programming to you. This is the homepage that I've written for you and it's written in HTML. HTML is a language that Web browsers use to read hypertext documents. It stands for HyperText Markup Language. It's a very simple computer language. In fact, it's so simple that it ranks closer to slang than language. Although this homepage in its present state is quite generic, you'll have plenty of opportunity at the end-of-chapter exercise to liven it up. I don't want you to do anything with it yet. I just want you to see what HTML looks like. We have many basics to discuss before you'll do anything reasonable with it.

Just to give you some idea of what other educators and their students have produced for their homepage, use the following URL:

http://web66.coled.umn.edu/schools.html

HTML

The gibberish that you saw on the template homepage in Appendix V is really pretty easy to understand. There are only a couple of things that you need to remember in order to read HTML. If you ignore the HTML gibberish that you don't quite understand, you'll see that the rest of the document makes sense. You can do this by alternately viewing your homepage file through your browser and then through your word processor. You don't need a fancy program to write HTML, just a word processor and an understanding of the code. Now look at the page with the gibberish. Notice that the HTML gibberish typically, but not always, comes in sets of two. At the very top you'll see a tag like this: <HTML>. A *tag* is an element of HTML code. It is added to the page to emphasize the text that will appear on the viewed Web page. Tags always have a angle bracket (<) at the beginning and an opposite angle bracket (>) at the end. Here are a couple of examples: <BODY>, <HEAD>, and <TITLE>. The other part of each tag set has a forward slash (/) preceding the word. Here are the other members of the tag pairs: </BODY>, </HEAD>, and </TITLE>. Tags, when used in sets or pairs, surround a section of text and define the beginning and end of an HTML section. Yes, it is possible to use tags incorrectly, just as it is possible to use English incorrectly. Here is an example of the basic HTML page that any properly coded page would conform to.

```
<HTML>
  <HEAD>
    This is where a description and purpose of the page is written.
    The material that is here is not intended to be viewed on the
    browser. It is only used to document the intent of the page.
  </HEAD>
  <BODY>
    This is where the material that is to be viewed through the
    browser will be written.
  </BODY>
</HTML>
```

All properly coded HTML documents are coded with this basic format. Notice the beginning and ending member of each tag pair. Although tags usually operate in pairs, some are used as solitary tags. Here are important examples of solitary tags that you should be aware of because they appear in your generic homepage. When you want to separate sections of text with two spaces you might use the paragraph tag, <P>. Two line break tags, <BR>, will also do the same thing. If you wanted the browser to make a horizontal line across the viewed page, then you would use a horizontal rule tag, <HR>. If you're paying attention to the tags, you'll notice that the tag names are abbreviations of what they do. Remember, you don't really have to absorb all this language stuff now. I made a link on your homepage that jumps you to several HTML resources.

Many other people have already written cool homepages and you could use theirs for a template if you don't like the one I wrote. One of the best things about writing HTML is that you really don't have to write it yourself. *Netscape* and many of the other browsers provide a great tool. If you select the *Source . . .* sub-menu under the *View* menu at the top of your screen, the actual HTML code of the page you are viewing will be displayed for you. All you have to do is find the cool and interesting things that others have done and copy the code and modify them to meet your personality.

Hyperlinks

One very important element in HTML is the code for hyperlinks (jumping points within Web pages). You know most of what you need to know to create hyperlinks. The HTML tag for a hyperlink is called an anchor

If you really want to jump into this HTML thing, then here are a number of resources that will help you go further. I have tried to find the resources that will be most beneficial to beginners. Some of these URLs may already be included on the homepage I created for you.

Global Network Navigator—Internet Resources

A wealth of information on HTML is located at this site. Included are links to beginning and advanced guides to HTML, sources for icons and graphics, indexes to reference guides, and lists of newsgroups devoted to discussion of the creation of HTML documents.

Web66 SharePages
This site contains numerous HTML pages, icons, clip art, and flags that can be downloaded and inserted into your HTML documents.

http://web66.coled.umn.edu/share/share.html

World Wide Web Consortium
One of the most complete and comprehensive sites for obtaining information on HTML. Located here are links to HTML reference manuals, web tools such as editors, information on access for the disabled, style sheets, reports and papers on the use of HTML, and lists of discussion groups and forums addressing HTML. Also included is a link to a validation service that quickly checks HTML documents.

http://www.w3.org/hypertext/www/markup.html

HTML Editors-Yahoo
Editors are an important tool to reduce the time in constructing an HTML document. These editors simplify the construction of HTML by allowing the user to click on buttons or menu items to insert, edit, and paste information. Many editors also have spelling checkers and some even check the syntax of your document. *Yahoo!* has a comprehensive list of editors for PC and Macintosh. Many of these editors have shareware versions that can be downloaded from this site.

**http://www.yahoo.com/computers_and_internet/
Internet/World_Wide_Web/html_editors/**

and it uses the tag pair <A> and </A>. There are two main components to an anchor tag. The first element is the URL and the second is the word. Here is an example of an anchor tag.

```
<A HREF="URL">
  Word
</A>
```

This is a little more than the <A> and </A> that I described earlier but it's still not that hard. I'll dismantle it for you and you can see how it works. The first line of the example above begins the code for an anchor. Notice again the <A>, but also notice that there is a lot more garbage thrown in between the A and the last angle bracket. You should also notice that this garbage is a URL. This URL tells the browser the location of the requested document. The second line is the text as it will appear on the HTML page (the button, so to speak). Because it will be a hypertext link, it will appear as a colored link by your browser. The anchor tag set is completed with the ending anchor tag, </A>. As it operates on an actual Web page, if the user selects the hypertext link, then the user will be sent the document specified by the URL.

Now for an exercise. Use your word processor and type in the basic page elements that I gave to you earlier (<HTML> and </HTML>). Within the body of the page I want you to type in an anchor tag set using a real URL. Use one or both of the examples provided below. Once you have this page, save it with the name TEST.HTML and view it with your browser.

A Beginners Guide to HTML
   http://www.ncsa.uiuc.edu/General/Internet/WWW/H
   TMLPrimer.html
How to Publish on the Web
   http://www.thegiim.org/

See step #2 in the following section for help in finding and displaying this file. Once you've got this page up and running on your browser, try the hyperlink. Does it work? You should notice that these URLs will take you to resources that will tell you more about Web publishing.

Home

So, you have a homepage, where do you put it to make it work? Well this depends on whether you will have access to a Web server or not. I'll assume that you don't and give you some instructions that will still help you use it to your advantage. Once you've completed your homepage, you'll have a file on either your hard drive or a floppy disk. The advantage of having your homepage on floppy disk is that you'll have a portable homepage that you can use on any computer. I'll give you a five-step procedure for finding and setting your default homepage to the one you've created.

1. *After* you finished the end-of-chapter exercise, you should copy your intended homepage to either a floppy disk or your hard drive.

2. With *Netscape* you should notice that there is a command under the *File* menu called *Open File . . . .* If you initiate this command, you'll get a dialog window where you can designate the file you wish to open. The trick to this is that this file isn't on a server. Select the HTML file from either your floppy drive or hard drive and press the Return key on your keyboard. Because your file is written in HTML your browser will open up and display it for you.

3. If it isn't set already, change your *Options* setting so that you can view the URLs of the pages that display on your browser. When this is set properly, you'll notice that your file's URL is listed something like this: file:///. . . . ./file.html. Notice that the protocol is not HTTP and that you may have more than two slashes.

4. Record this URL on a piece of paper so that you can refer to it in the next step. I would ask you to remember it and copy it to step 5 but every little slash and colon is important. So, this will save you from a possible SNAFU (Situation Normal. All Fouled Up. I learned this from a friend in the Army).

5. If you remember from earlier in this chapter, I described how you can change the homepage designation for your browser. Go back to this section and use the description to open the *Preferences* section of the *Options* menu. Open the preference for *Windows and Links* and enter the URL that you wrote down from step 4 into the homepage entry window.

Now that you've performed these steps, your browser should automatically jump you onto your homepage when you select the Home button from the toolbar. Give it a try. The procedures that you've just performed have allowed your browser to memorize the location of your homepage file. If you move it or erase it, then you'll have to do this all over again. Builds character—right?

Run Wild

There are many more tags than I have the space to describe here for you, or for that matter, than you probably want to know right now. They are not hard to learn, and in fact, there are places on the Web that offer on-line tutorials on HTML design. Once you have your homepage operational, you'll see that I included links to some of these places for you. As you learn more about the Internet, the Web, and HTML, you'll discover ways to add pictures to your pages. Later you'll even begin adding sounds and maybe a video clip or two. We are at the beginning of a new way of learning and communicating. The tools available to you at this moment are only a hint of what will be available to you in a year. If I could give you one bit of advice on your journeys through this new world, this World Wide Web, it would be to *watch*, *look*, and *listen* to your world.

Make Yourself at Home!

The activity of the day is to make your own homepage with bookmarks. One of the greatest problems that I have, as a teacher and administrator of a student network, is the gradual and insidious buildup of cluttersome bookmarks. The situation is obvious: each student changes the browsers on the computers in my classroom to meet his or her personal needs. I never know what to expect when I need to teach a class or use a browser. Students, with much less experience, are confused and disoriented. I have, to some extent, come up with a solution.

The gibberish that you will see in Appendix V is my solution. It is a template for a student homepage to be kept on a floppy disk. The added value in this is that you can also use this generic homepage as a portable resource disk on most networked computers. Still the only drawback is that you can't jump between Macintosh and Windows with this arrangement. But then, I'll leave that up to the computer giants.

You should know a couple of conventions so that you will understand what you need to do. I have used a *large italic font* to represent the text that you are to replace with your information. HTML tags are represented in a <SMALLER FONT, ALL IN UPPER-CASE AND WITH ANGLE BRACKETS>. Text that is not an HTML tag and *does not* need to be changed is in a regular size and font.

To create a homepage on a floppy disk simply use any word processor to type the following information onto a floppy disk. Give the file a name with the suffix html (HOMENAME.HTML). Once this is done, you should follow the instructions in section 3.3 to adapt it to your liking. Remember to show some style and personality!

It's All Greek to Me

•••••••

Glossary

Archie   This is a search tool used to find resources that are stored on Internet-based FTP servers. Contrary to what I said earlier in the manual, Archie is short for Archive because it performs an archive search for resources. (see FTP and Server)

AVI   This stands for Audio/Video Interleaved. It is a Microsoft Corporation format for encoding video and audio for digital transmission.

Background   This refers to an image or color that is present in the background of a viewed Web document. Complex images are becoming very popular as backgrounds but require a great deal more time to download. The color of default background can be set for most Web browsers.

Bookmark   This refers to a list of URLs saved within a browser. The user can edit and modify the bookmark list to add and delete URLs as the user's interests change. Bookmark is a term used by *Netscape* to refer to the user's list of URLs while 'Hotlist' is used by *Mosaic* to refer to the same list. (see Hotlist, *Mosaic,* and URL)

Browser   This is a software program that is used to view and browse information on the Internet. Browsers are also referred to as clients. (see Client)

Bulletin Board Service   This is an electronic bulletin board. It is sometimes referred to as a BBS. Information on a BBS is posted to a computer where many can dial in and read it and/or comment on it. BBSs may or may not be connected to the Internet. Some are accessible by modem dial-in only.

Cache   This refers to a section of memory that is set aside to store information that is commonly used by the computer or an active piece of software. Most browsers will create a cache to commonly accessed images. An example might be the images that are common to the user's homepage. Retrieving images from the cache is much quicker than downloading the images from the original source each time they are required.

Clickable image (Clickable map)   This refers to an interface used in Web documents that allows the user to click or select different areas of an image and receive different responses. Clickable images are becoming very common as a way of offering a user many different selections within a common visual format.

Client   This is a software program used to view information from remote computers. Clients function in a Client-Server information exchange model. This term may also be loosely applied to the computer that is used to request information from the server. (see Server)

Compressed file   This refers to a file or document that has been compacted to save memory space so that it can be easily and quickly transferred through the Internet.

Download   This is the process of transferring a file, document, or program from a remote computer to a local computer. (see Upload)

E-mail   This is the short name for electronic mail. E-mail is sent electronically from one person to another. Some companies have e-mail systems that are not part of the Internet. E-mail can also be sent to one person or to many different people. I sometimes refer to this as JunkE-mail. You form your own opinions.

FAQ   This stands for Frequently Asked Questions. An FAQ is a file or document where a moderator or administrator will post commonly asked questions and their answers. Although it is very easy to communicate across the Internet, if you have a question, you should check for the answer in an FAQ first.

Forms   This refers to an interface element used within Web documents to allow a user to send information back to a Web server. With a forms interface, the user is requested to type responses within entry windows to be returned to the server for processing. Forms rely on a server computer to process the submittals. They are becoming more common as browser and server software improve.

FTP   This stands for File Transfer Protocol. It is a procedure used to transfer large files and programs from one computer to another. Access to the computer to transfer files may or may not require a password. Some FTP servers are set up to allow public access by anonymous log-on. This process is referred to as *Anonymous FTP*.

GIF   This stands for Graphics Interchange Format. It is a format created by CompuServe to allow electronic transfer of digital images. GIF files are a common and much used format and can be viewed by both Mac and Windows users.

Gopher   This is a format structure and resource for providing information on the Internet. It was created at the University of Minnesota.

GUI   An acronym for Graphical User Interface. It is a combination of the appearance and the method of interacting with a computer. A GUI requires the use of a mouse to select commands on an icon based monitor screen. Macintosh and Windows operating systems are typical GUI examples.

Homepage   In its specific sense, this refers to a Web document that a browser loads as its central navigational point to browse the Internet. It may also be used to refer to a Web page describing an individual. In the most general sense, it is used to refer to any Web document.

Hotlist   This is a list of URLs saved within the *Mosaic* Web browser. This same list is referred to as a Bookmark within the *Netscape* Web browser.

HTML   An abbreviation for HyperText Markup Language, the common language used to write documents that appear on the World Wide Web.

HTTP   An abbreviation for HyperText Transport Protocol, the common protocol used to communicate between World Wide Web servers.

Hypertext   This refers to text elements within a document that have an embedded connection to another item. Web documents use hypertext links to access documents, images, sounds, and video files from the Internet. The term hyperlink is a general term that applies to elements on Web pages other than text.

Inline image   This refers to images that are viewed along with text on Web documents. All inline images are in the GIF format. JPEG format is the other common image format for Web documents, but an external viewer is typically required to view them.

JPEG   This stands for Joint Photographic Experts Group. It is also commonly used to refer to a format used to transfer digital images.

Jughead   This is a service for performing searches on the Internet. (see *Archie* and *Veronica*)

Mosaic   This is the name of the browser that was created at the National Center for Supercomputing Applications. It was the first Web browser to have a consistent interface for the Macintosh, Windows, and UNIX environments. The success of this browser is really responsible for the expansion of the Web.

MPEG   This stands for Motion Picture Experts Group. It is also a format used to make, view, and transfer both digital audio and digital video files.

Newsgroup This is the name for the discussion groups that can be on the Usenet. Not all newsgroups are accessible through the Internet. Some are accessible only through a modem connection.

QuickTime This is a format used by Apple Computer to make, view, edit, and send digital audio and video.

Server This is a software program used to provide, or serve, information to remote computers. Servers function in a Client-Server information exchange model. This term may also be loosely applied to the computer that is used to serve the information. (see Client)

Table This refers to a specific formatting element found in HTML pages. Tables are used on HTML documents to visually organize information.

Telnet This is the process of remotely connecting and using a computer at a distant location.

Upload This is the process of moving or transferring a document, file, or program from one computer to another computer.

URL This is an abbreviation for Uniform Resource Locator. In its basic sense it is an address used by people on the Internet to locate documents. URLs take a common format that describes the protocol for information transfer, the host computer address, path to the desired file, and the name of the file requested.

Usenet This is a world-wide system of discussion groups, also called newsgroups. There are many thousand newsgroups but only a percentage are accessible from the Internet.

Veronica Believe it or not, this is an acronym. It stands for Very Easy Rodent Oriented Net-wide Index to Computerized Archives. This is a database of menu names from a large number of Gopher servers. It is a quick and easy way to search Gopher resources for information by keyword. It was developed at the University of Nevada.

WAIS This stands for Wide Area Information Servers. This is a software package that allows the searching of large indexes of information from the Internet.

WAV This stands for Waveform sound format. It is a Microsoft Corporation format for encoding sound files.

Web (WWW) This stands for the World Wide Web. When loosely applied, this term refers to the Internet and all of its associated incarnations such as Gopher, FTP, HTTP, etc. More specifically, this term refers to a subset of the servers on the Internet that use HTTP to transfer hyperlinked documents in a page-like format.

Appendix I
What's Under The Hood?

•••••••

Basic Components

Here is a computer question to get your mind working. What is the difference between a Corvette and a Chevette? Okay, it's a stupid question but give it some consideration. The difference is a couple thousand dollars. Everything else is just fluff, mileage, and auto insurance. But, if we break this down to our basic needs (if we really need a ride) both cars are the same. The same goes for computers and networks. The simple nogloss stuff will get you by while saving you money; and the high-gloss stuff will transform your cash into dash and make your Internet browsing a little more enjoyable. Many of you may be lucky enough to have computers on your campus that are set up to allow Internet access. In case you don't, I'll list the *minimum* systems, connections, and services that you'll need to enter the Internet, but you'll have to decide how shiny your system needs to be.

The Computer

Now watch how you approach this issue if you ask for advice on which computer platform to buy. Opinions are known to run a little hot with some people when they begin to argue the differences between Macintosh and PC-compatible systems. Proponents from both camps can easily get out of hand. If they begin to foam at the mouth, then you know you're in for a real adventure. The best advice that I can give to you is test them both at a computer store. Choose the one that you can pay for and are most comfortable using. After all, it won't do you any good if you don't enjoy using it or if it gets repossessed halfway through the semester.

These are the **minimum** system configurations that you'll need.

Macintosh	PC-Compatible
68020	Intel 486
System 7.0	Windows 3.1
256 color monitor	VGA monitor
8 MB of RAM	8 MB of RAM
5 MB of disk space	5 MB of disk space

The Internet Connection

If you get lucky, your campus has already recognized the importance of the Internet as a teaching and learning tool. If the equipment is set up, then they should have Internet, or more specifically Web access ready to go. Okay, if you didn't enroll in a campus with vision, bucks, or both, then you'll have to do it the hard way. There are many resources that can help you set up a connection from home.

Some campuses, although lacking a walk-in lab, have made arrangements for students to dial into the campus computer system and hopefully the Internet with a modem. If such is the case, then search out the campus computer hack and ask for help. This may require a fair deal of begging, bribing, or borrowing.

Another option for accessing the Internet is to subscribe to a company such as America Online, CompuServe, Delphi, eWorld, Prodigy, or Microsoft. Many other companies are also in business to sell you access to the Internet and you should consider them in addition to these. Some of these on-line service providers advertise the availability of access. However, you are required to use their software and it may not have all of the options that you might want. As always, it is a buyer's market and you should shop around and test drive everything before you buy.

When it comes to buying modems, I suggest you buy a 28.8K baud modem. A baud is a measure of the speed with which the modem transfers data. The higher the number, usually the faster the transfer rate. With a typical 28.8K baud modem you can expect that it will take a few seconds to transfer a typical Web page, but this will vary depending on the complexity of the page.

The Browser Software

If everything has fallen into place, you should now have access to a computer with muscle and a gateway to the Internet, either through your school or an Internet service provider. But you're missing one very important piece, the Web client software. A more descriptive name for this software is *browser*, as that is what most people do with it. It is used to browse or wander, sometimes aimlessly, through the Internet.

There are many Web browsers on the market and in the space of time that it has taken me to write this manual I would not doubt that several more have entered the race to capture your dollar. The mother of all browsers is *Netscape Navigator*, now in version 2.01, but there are a number of other browsers available. I have included a list of many of the available browsers in Appendix II. You should really evaluate them all and choose the one that you're most comfortable with. Browsers are typically very cheap, if not simply free for educational use. (Considering the nature of my audience, I should give proper reverence to that last statement.) *Netscape, Mosaic,* and many of the other browsers are FREE for student use! So, don't be afraid to evaluate them all.

Now, if you have all of these basic elements and they've been put together correctly, you should be ready to surf! Enjoy!

Appendix II
Eyeglasses and Spyglasses

•••••••

Web Browsers

Emissary Desktop
Wolllongong Co.
1129 San Antonio Road
Palo Alto, CA 94303
800-872-8649
415-962-7100

Explore Internet
FTP Software Co.
100 Brickstone Sq. 5 Fl.
Andover, MA 01810
800-282-4387
508-685-3300

IBM Internet Connection
for Windows
IBM Corp.
Dept. G90
PO Box 12195
Research Triangle Park
NC 27709
800-CallIBM

Internet Chameleon
10725 N. De Anza Blvd.
Cupertino, CA 95014
408-973-7171

Internet in a Box
CompuServe
316 Occidental Ave. S.
Seattle, WA 98104
800-777-9638
206-447-0300

Netscape Navigator
Netscape Corp.
501 E. Middlefield Rd.
Mountain View, CA 94043
415-528-2555

Superhighway Access
Frontier Technology
10201 N. Port Washington Rd.
Mequon, WI 53092
800-929-3054
414-241-4555

Appendix III
A Call to Order

• • • • • • •

Internet Providers

America Online
America Online Inc.
8619 Westwood Center Dr.
Vienna, VA 22182-2285
800-827-6364
703-448-8700
aohotline@aol.com

CompuServe
CompuServe Inc.
5000 Arlington Centre Blvd.
Columbus, OH 43220
800-487-9197
614-457-8600
70006,101@compuserve.com

Delphi
Delphi Internet Services Corp.
1030 Massachusetts Ave.
Cambridge, MA 02138
800-695-4005
617-491-3393
617-491-4903 fax
sales@delphi.com

Prodigy
Prodigy Services Co.
445 Hamilton Ave.
White Plains, NY 10601
800-776-3449

If you don't want to use one of these large service providers but would prefer a company that drops the frills and gives you direct access to the Internet, you can locate such service providers at this Web address:

(http://www.celestin.com/pocia/)

Just search by the area code for your phone service and you'll get a list of providers that will accept your money to use their service.

Appendix IV
It's News to Me

•••••••

Education Newsgroups

Think of this as a starter kit to Education groups on the Usenet. This is not a complete list and some of the newsgroups that I've listed will, without a doubt, disappear in the near future. Additionally, there will be many new groups born in this same time period. One of them might even be yours. As I've said before, it's a changing world.

The names are very descriptive for the topic of discussion. You will find that some are very interesting and some are not. Subscribe to several of the groups and eavesdrop on their conversations for awhile before you jump in. This will give you some experience with the general attitude of the group and prevent some embarrassment on your part. I also suggest that you read the FAQ and any postings directed to new participants to the group.

k12.chat.elementary   casual conversation for elementary students, grades K–5.

k12.chat.junior   casual conversation for students in grades 6–8.

k12.chat.senior   casual conversation for high school students.

k12.chat.teacher   casual conversation for teachers grades K–12.

k12.ed.art   arts and craft curricula in K–12 education

k12.ed.business   business educational curricula in grades K–12.

k12.ed.comp.literacy   teaching computer literacy in grades K–12.

k12.ed.health-pe   health and physical education curricula in grades K–12.

k12.ed.life-skills   home economics, career education and school counseling

k12.ed.math   mathematics curriculum in K–12 education

k12.ed.music   music education and performing arts curriculum in grades K–12

k12.ed.science   science curriculum for grades K–12

k12.ed.soc-studies   geography, civics, political science, and history curriculum for K–12.

k12.ed.special   education of students with special needs

k12.ed.tag   K–12 curriculum for gifted and talented students

k12.ed.tech   industrial arts and vocational education

k12.lang.art   language arts (reading, writing, literature) instruction

k12.lang.deutsch-eng   bilingual German/English practice with native speakers

k12.lang.esp-eng   bilingual Spanish/English practice with native speakers

k12.lang.francais   French practice with native speakers

k12.lang.russian   bilingual Russian/English practice with native speakers

k12.library   implementing information technology in school libraries

k12.sys.ch0 (through ch12)   current projects

k12.sys.projects   potential projects

Appendix V
Stepping Out

• • • • • • •

Student Homepage Template

```
<HTML>
<HEAD>
  <TITLE>Your Home Page</TITLE>
</HEAD>

<BODY>
<CENTER>
  <H1>Your Name</H1>
  <H2>Your Title, Major, or Philosophy</H2>
  <H3>
  <ADDRESS>
    Your address<BR>
    May<BR>
    Go<BR>
    Here<BR>
    <P>
    Your e-mail address<BR>
  </ADDRESS>
  </H3>
</CENTER>
<HR>

<DL>
  <H2>This Is Your Life:</H2>
```

\<DD>*Just say something about yourself. After you've added something to your homepage file compare it to what actually shows on your browser. You'll notice that most of this gibberish is not visible.*
\<P>
\<DD>*You can have as many paragraphs as you wish. Here's another. Enjoy.*
\<P>
\</DL>

\<DL>
  \<H2>Important Educational Resources**\</H2>**
  \<DD>

    \<A HREF="http://www.execpc.com/~hughes">
    Internet for Educators Resources
  \</A>
\</DL>
\<HR>
\<DL>
  \<H2>Handbooks and Manuals**\</H2>**
  \<DD>
    \<A HREF="http://www.matisse.net/files/glossary.html">
    Glossary of Internet Terms
  \</A>
  \<DD>
    \<A HREF="http://www.cdtl.umn.edu/eudora_http/contents.html">
    Eudora Manual
  \</A>
  \<DD>
    \<A HREF="http://home.netscape.com/eng/mozilla/1.1/handbook/">
    Netscape Handbook
  \</A>
\</DL>
\<HR>
\<DL>
  \<H2>Directories and Search Engines:**\</H2>**
  \<DD>
    \<A HREF="http://flosun.salk.edu/cusi.html">

```
                    CUSI Search Clearinghouse
            </A>
        <DD>
            <A HREF="http://altavista.digital.com/">
                AltaVista Search Engine
            </A>
        <DD>
            <A HREF="http://www.yahoo.com/">
                Yahoo Directory
            </A>
    </DL>
    <HR>
    <DL>
        <H2>Design and Publish:</H2>
        <DD>
            <A HREF="http://www.ncsa.uiuc.edu/General/Internet/WWW
            /HTMLPrimer.html">
                A Beginner's Guide to HTML
            </A>
        <DD>
            <A HREF="http://www.access.digex.net/~werbach
            /barebone.html">
                The BareBones Guide to HTML
            </A>
        <DD>
            <A HREF="http://www.thegiim.org/">
                How to Publish On The Web
            </A>
    </DL>
    <HR>
    <H3>
            Your Name<A HREF="mailto:Name@server.edu">E-mail
            address</A>
    </H3>

    </BODY>
    </HTML>
```